no idea
what
I'm doing
but f*ck it

ron lim

THOUGHT
CATALOG
Books

THOUGHTCATALOG.COM

Published by Thought Catalog Books, an imprint of Thought Catalog, a digital magazine owned and operated by The Thought & Expression Co. Inc., an independent media organization founded in 2010 and based in the United States of America. For stocking inquiries, contact stockists@shopcatalog.com.

Produced by Chris Lavergne and Noelle Beams
Art direction and design by KJ Parish
Circulation management by Isidoros Karamitopoulos

thoughtcatalog.com | shopcatalog.com

Second Edition, Limited Edition Pressing
Printed in the United States of America

ISBN 978-1-949759-59-4

chapters

what this book is about

I want this book to be something that people can use as motivation to take that little leap out. growing up, we all have a little vision in our mind of what life could potentially be. but as we get older, our dreams are dulled by the standards of society. you become uncertain of the vision you used to be so sure about. and over time, you start to doubt yourself more and more and you are now unsure if you should ever make that leap. you think there is hope, but you are not so sure anymore. I want this book to help others believe that the "vision" they have is realistic, and not a fantasy. it is there. but just because it's there doesn't mean that people are going to get it the moment they reach for it. it just means that it is there. and they can decide what they want to do with that hope. I want this book to be a reassurance for people that it is okay to not know what you are doing. you don't need to know what you are doing. no one knows what they are doing. it is the doing that makes all the difference, not the knowing. I want this book to give people the bit of courage they need to take the next step out. I want this book to be the support for people who feel like they have no support. I want this book to be the living proof that you don't need to know what you are doing to get things done, like me writing this book.

no one

knows

anything

no one knows anything.

not you. not me. not your parents. not your friends.

but yet we are all stuck in this illusion that
somehow everyone knows everything.

everyone, but you.

and that seems to put you in a bad place. because
now you feel like you are inferior to everyone else.
and you should somehow have known better.

no idea how, but somehow.

the funny thing is – everyone is thinking the same thing.

you don't know
what you are doing
so you look for answers
in other people
but the truth is,
nobody really knows
what they are doing either
and instead of letting someone
who has no idea
tell you what to do
why not just fuck it up yourself
anyway?

you disappoint yourself
when you give something
and wait
for the same thing back.

you know.

but you act like you don't.

you want something.

but you talk yourself out of it.

you say it's over.

but you still hold onto it.

you dream of one thing.

but you do another.

and yet, you wonder why you never get there.

a regret:

you can't decide
which choice to go for
so you end up
doing nothing at all.

I think growth
is meant to be
confusing,
because
if you're not questioning
then how
are you finding out?

you say you don't care
but yet you still do
you know the things
you shouldn't do
but yet you still do.

you see yourself
in an endless cycle
with no meaning around
you tell yourself that
you shouldn't stay in it any longer
but yet you still do
another round and round and round.

you don't know
what you are waiting for
so you are just waiting
for something
that isn't going to come.

you're waiting for the right timing.

but are you being logical?

you're waiting for a perfect time – where
everything will work out smoothly.

but there is no perfect time. and the "perfection" you're
waiting for might not be as perfect as you think.

there might come a time in the future where your
problems will become less of a problem.

with enough time, problems sometimes
start to solve themselves.

but is that really perfect?

what about all the time you give up in between,
while waiting for things to be "perfect"?

you want to keep everything, but you can't. you are afraid
to make a wrong decision, so you avoid doing anything.

you wait for a perfect time, but you end up losing
all the time in between. is that really still perfect?

the biggest mistake
you can make
is to keep waiting
when it doesn't
change anything.

we hear the most
from the things
people don't say.

if you spend your energy
trying to change things
you can't change,
you will only end up
being depleted
for absolutely no reason.

you say
you want to be special
but yet when you get
an epiphany
you choose to ignore it
and be like everyone else.

how many times
have you ignored your intuition
because you were too afraid
of what someone else
might think?

say yes to the things you want to say yes to. we come across opportunities that excite us every now and then. and sometimes we are too passive to say yes, and they are gone before we know it. you can't know if it will work out. but you can't know anything at all if you never say yes to anything.

how different would your life be if you did
all the things you told yourself you would?

the energy you spend
worrying about your future
is the same energy you need
to do something
about the present.

3 things to say yes to:

1. say yes to trying something new. step just an inch out. try something new that doesn't take much of your time and effort. you never know – the new exposure could be what you need to make an eventual shift towards the better.

2. say yes to leaving behind situations that don't work anymore. you can't hold onto something that doesn't work or there will never be room for something that does.

3. say yes to reinventing yourself. the whole point of getting new exposure is so that you can make a behavioral shift. if you confine yourself to this "perception" people have of you, then you will always be the same person.

it is the easiest thing
to simply
just do nothing at all
and that is why most people
will not make it.

how many losses
did you take
without even trying
only to find out later that
someone else
has gotten to where you want
by doing the exact same things
you had in mind?

you keep thinking
to yourself
that you are never
going to make it
and that is why
you will never make it.

you manifest
a negative thought
inside you
on repeat
until it comes true
and you call it
bad luck.

someone asked me this the other day — *"how
do you know what to chase after?"*

and honestly,

you don't.

the truth is — you don't know.

if the thought of something makes you
very excited, chase after it.

if there is something you have in mind that you
can't stop thinking about, chase after it.

but you never really know what the right answer is.

because there isn't one.

you won't know if it's right until you have the answer.
and you can't get an answer if you don't try.

honestly, I don't really know what I should
chase after either. but you should chase
anyway. because that's how you find out.

you wait for others
to point you in a direction
and you wonder why
you end up in a place
you don't belong.

are you searching
for an answer
from other people
that only exists
in yourself?

I do not know
where I am meant to be
but I do know
that I do not belong here
and that is enough
for me to leave.

leave
if you
feel like
shit

the first time you leave is the hardest.

letting go of things you were holding on to so closely
that you didn't know if you still wanted them anymore.

convincing yourself that you need to take a different
path because you've been feeling stuck for too long.

and then hesitating. because what if it doesn't work out?

you know you need to leave...eventually.

but what if this is not the right time? what
if the right time has already passed? there is
no way to tell what the right answer is.

but how long can you hold on until you can't anymore?

you will never be happy
if you continue to repeat
the same few things
that make you feel like shit.

you gotta start living for yourself. do the things you want to do. come up with new ideas. make changes. just. try. stuff. fuck it up a few times. whatever. you will still be alive anyway.

leaving
felt like the most foreign thing
until you are in a foreign place
far away from home
and you realize that home
was never where you want to be
in the first place.

it's easy to leave
when things are shit
when it's obvious
that it's time to go

but how do you leave
when things are not the best
but nothing is horribly wrong
you've tried tolerating
but you've been tolerating for a long time
and you probably could some more
but you really don't want to anymore

if you leave
they will paint you a villain
if you stay
you're condemning yourself
to a death sentence

tell me
how do you leave
when nothing is too fucked up yet
but the one feeling especially fucked up
is you

everything is okay.

but I want so much more than okay.

you break your own heart
by telling yourself
to give it another shot
when you already know
it is time to let go.

make a change.

you can always go back to what you've left behind.

chances are, you probably won't want to go back once you make a leap forward. but yet, you spend the vast majority of your energy debating if you should take a leap.

that's the thing about us as humans – we are good at moving forward. we intuitively try to move forward in whatever circumstances we are put in.

when you put yourself in an environment with tremendous upside to grow, you will intuitively figure out a way to get there.

but if you trap yourself in an environment where you are already done growing, then there really isn't anything much left for you to do.

if you're debating with yourself if you should make a change, the answer is yes. you can always go back to what you've left behind.

you've got yourself
and that's all you need
to make a change.

it is better to fuck up
than to live your entire life
and have nothing
happen at all.

there is a kind of tiredness
that sleep doesn't make go away
it comes from the aching of your soul
longing to be someone else
tired of pretending to care about
all the things you don't care about.

there is a kind of tiredness
you cannot make go away
it lays there deep in your soul
growing more and more weary
as you continue to do things
that do not feed your soul.

how many times
do you need
to go back and forth
to make up that decision
you've known all along?

anywhere
is the right direction
if you don't care
where you are going.

if you wait for too long,
it won't be the same
anymore.

at sixteen years old,
fear is not being able to fit in
not funny enough
not skinny enough
not smart enough
not having enough friends
or no one to hang out with
fear is staying at home
when you wanted to be out

at nineteen years old,
fear is leaving your comfort zone
wanting to try something new
but having no one to do it with
and being too afraid to try it alone
fear is having friends say yes
and backing out the last minute

at twenty two years old,
fear is being stuck in the same routine
being in a place you wanted to get out
since you were before sixteen
fear is not trying enough
when you were younger
and probably making the same mistakes
because you are still afraid

at twenty five years old,
fear is being as lost as ever
you're clearly an adult now
why does nothing still make sense?
fear is never being enough
never ending up anywhere
because you don't know where to be
fear is finally trying the ideas
you've always had in your head
and still ending up
in the same old place

what are you more afraid of
is it really change
or things
staying the same?

stop giving your energy to people
who make you feel like shit.

let go of what's holding you back. let go of the people who have already cut you out of their lives. let go of the routines that no longer serve you any purpose. let go of the things you chose when you were unsure and have now lost excitement for. you are holding on to more than what you need and you need to make room to grow.

sometimes
the best thing
you can do for yourself
is to leave.

3 things leaving taught me:

1. change is possible. maybe things will suck at the beginning but you will feel happier. and that's better.

2. you're stuck because you're afraid that you will never have it as good as you do now. but that's not true. you've out-done yourself plenty of times before. you can and will do it again.

3. you learn more quickly by making mistakes than trying to avoid them. don't overthink. do what you feel is right. if you make a mistake, you can always fix it.

at the end of it all
the biggest obstacle
still remains
to be yourself.

the other day
someone asked me
how do you make it so easy
leaving everything behind
and go
just like that.

I thought for a minute
and to that I answered,
when you run out of reasons to stay
and your soul is pulling you to go
you would know,
and that
is the time to go.

if there is anything
leaving has taught me
it is that
change is more possible
than we think.

it's better to be lost
than in a place
you don't want to be in.

there will come a time
when it is time to leave
don't rush it
if you are not there yet
you don't need to leave now
but when the time comes,
take a deep breath
and get the fuck out of there.

sometimes
the best self-care thing
you can do for yourself
is to not care.

you grow older and some things are just not
the same anymore.

places that once felt like home can no
longer contain your ambition.

people you still have love for no longer
want the same things as you do.

you don't have to shrink yourself to fit in
places you have outgrown.

life is not meant to be lived in one area.

make

your own

mistakes

it only has to make sense to you.

not anybody else.

if it makes you happy, it is a good enough reason to do it.

if you think that it is what you need, it
is a good enough reason to do it.

it doesn't matter if others don't agree, they are not you.

make your own mistakes.

what is the one thing you would
do if you weren't so afraid?

I'm ready for my life to change.

move to a new country. find a new routine to commit to. jump onto any opportunities that excite me. have coffee with strangers and tell each other our life stories. change up my personality. be a little more adventurous or outgoing than I normally would. pick up a new hobby. learn surfing. start going to the gym. drink kombucha. turmeric juice. film my new life and document it down. write out my thoughts and post them on the internet. meet strangers on the internet. make time to be creative. work on my ideas. make these ideas come to life. fuck shit up. try again. and again. repeat repeat repeat.

it's always
the choices
you didn't make
that come back
to haunt you.

the first time is the hardest.

like the first time you drive a car.

or the first time you jump into a pool from 10 feet above.

or the first time you decide to travel entirely on your own.

or the first time you walk up to someone and say hi.

it feels terribly foreign and difficult. until you do it once.

and then you laugh at yourself for being ever so afraid. and for taking so long to overcome something that you now find so casual.

we spend time dwelling in our own personal barriers and sometimes we get stuck in it for way too long.

there is fear. but it's not always directed at the circumstances. sometimes the fear is just something you build up in your own head and then it becomes something you have to overcome.

you create a battle within a battle you have going on and you spend time trying to fight the battle you've created instead of the one you're supposed to fight.

it's a twisted logic but yet it still happens all the time.

you don't always have to
get it right the first time.

here's a thought.

instead of second guessing if what you did
was right, why not just do more?

contemplating a decision you've made takes energy.

doing more takes energy too.

the difference is that — one is a dead
end, the other one is limitless.

oftentimes, you are in control more than you know.

you get to choose where you want to put your energy.

make your own mistakes,
deal with the consequences
of your own decisions.

people change
just like how you are
no longer the same person
you were two years ago

your past
does not define you
if you fuck up
you can always get back up

some days
feel like years
and sometimes years
can happen in a few days

nothing happens
and then it does
all at once

it's okay
if you change your mind
or do the wrong things twice
you live and you learn
and that's just how it is sometimes

two choices.

both are good.

but you can't do both.

and you can't decide which one you should go for.

there is no wrong choice here.

anything you do will be right.

the only mistake you can make is if you don't
make a decision and you end up having neither.

you can't choose wrong because you can't choose both.

you make a choice and you live with
it and you never look back.

there will be many more choices down the
road that you will have to make.

and you will have to make these choices. if
you want to keep moving forward.

if you're stuck with two choices, pick one.

do everything you can to make it work.

and if it doesn't work, come back again and
pick the other one. if opportunity allows.

if not, you live with it and you learn.
and you keep looking forward.

there will always be more choices to make.

give it some time.

stick with the decision you have chosen
and just let things play out.

let yourself live through the process.

you don't have to evaluate things right after you
make the decision. you won't know it so quickly.

let life happen. and let yourself live for a little.

there is a certain kind of power that comes with fully accepting your circumstances for what they are. knowing that you can't change the situation in this immediate moment, but it doesn't mean that it will always be this way. knowing that you have the power in you to change things, but it takes time. and if anything, time and effort are two of the things you have in you to give. and understanding that with enough effort and time, you can change anything. it is all within your control.

the worst thing
you can do
when you're stuck
with two excellent choices
is to choose neither
because you can't
make up your mind.

I've always thought I'd go back
if I ever had the chance to
but I won't
not because I don't want to
because I do,
but I won't

there is a line
between knowing what you want
and what you need
and very often,
they are not the same thing

we make mistakes
and life goes on
we don't always choose right
and life goes on
sometimes we do everything right
still it doesn't work out anyway
and life goes on
and life goes on

isn't it interesting
how we always regret
the things we didn't do
and rarely the ones
we did?

don't make the mistake
of making mistakes
based on
somebody else's terms.

you gotta get the bad days out. the days you spend sitting in bed wishing you could be elsewhere but there is nowhere else you want to be. the days where creativity just doesn't flow. the days where you try to make plans and they all end up being canceled. the days where people are just not available and things just don't work out. you gotta get those days out. bad days come and bad days go. it's like going through a deck of cards. you gotta get the bad ones out to make space so you can draw the good ones again.

let yourself flow
towards where
you want to be

life is always flowing
you either flow with it
or you flow against it

neither direction is correct
and neither is wrong
you just want to be flowing
as much as you can

get out.
make mistakes.
do something different.

live the dream
you have always wanted
when you were younger.

the dream that
you have been spending
your whole life
thinking about.

do it once.
it's okay to fail.
it's not about succeeding.
it's about living a dream
you have always wanted.

do it once.
do it before
your life is over.

remember, you only fail when you give up.

otherwise, it's only a process of getting there.

it's like you're lost and trying to find the right
directions to get to your destination.

you're not a failure for being lost. you just need to find
the right direction and then start walking towards it.

you are here right now. and you want to be somewhere else. there is a gap between where you are currently, and where you want to be. closing the gap is what motivates me the most.

at some point
you just gotta take a leap
and live with the consequences
of the decision you made.

trying to be
a little comfortable
with the things
that make me uncomfortable
so I can be a little better.

some days feel a little
heavier than the rest
but you will always
have time to breathe
and try again.

go where you feel
the most appreciated
or until then,
go figure it out
on your own.

do the things you have in mind.

especially if you have been thinking about it for a long time.

we spend too much time "waiting".

but what are we really waiting for?

waiting till you have a backup plan? waiting for someone
to do it with? just simply waiting to see how it goes?

or have you been waiting for so long that
you forgot what you are waiting for?

you don't have to do it all at once. take baby steps out.

but don't forget to do the things you have in
mind. don't end up waiting in vain.

there is
a big world
out there

I want to dedicate this chapter
to tell the story of me leaving
how one thought
led to another
a childhood vision
repeated throughout the years
how I lived my life
looking forward to the day
I get my freedom
my entire existence
leading up to that one singular moment
but still,
I was uncertain
but the thought to not do something
I spent an entire lifetime thinking about
was unbearable
so I had to
for my childhood,
for all the years I wished I was somewhere else
for my future
for myself

— no idea what I'm doing but fuck it

pack your bags
buy a one-way ticket
leave
if you feel like shit

all alone
with everywhere to go
but no plans at all,
what should I do next?

people seem to think of "the leap" as
this destination that they are chasing.

but in reality, "the leap" is not a destination.

it is not even close to the destination.

"the leap" is the beginning.

it is the beginning of all things new.

you get to decide what you want
to be. where you want to go.

but this time, on your own terms.

you can spend a long time
wishing for one thing to happen
and when it finally does
make sure you claim it.

earth with a little bit of fire
grounded all my life but
always yearning for something wild
I'm nothing but an inspiration
of all my favorite songs

wrote a vision for my life
and sold my soul for it
the process is excruciating sometimes
but the pain is pleasure
I spent a long time wondering if I'm able to feel
but now I know I do

someday, someday
the spaces between will be filled
and I hope for that before I disintegrate
maybe I'll stop beating myself up
while my heart is still beating

it feels incomplete
and maybe it always will be
silently, the false hopes come and go
and I'Il still make it up as I go
this will end when it's complete
or when it reaches the end

it wasn't until I left
that I finally realized
that being away in a foreign place
with no idea of where to go
was actually
what I needed the most.

people find you
confusing
because
there's a thousand different versions
in your head
you're trying to live through
never stuck in the same box twice
always seeking for something else
you are
ever-changing
and that is what most people
can't comprehend.

make space
for the things
that make your heart
beat a little faster.

I was a child
when I wanted to leave
go live anywhere in the world
I just wanted to get out of here

fourteen year old me
couldn't do shit
didn't know shit
all I knew was that
I didn't want to spend my life in this box
there is a big world out there
and I want to see it

the process feels like a long time
when your day to day looks the same
someday I will make it out
life is not meant to be lived in one place

time takes time
and it's funny when I think about it sometimes
how that one little idea you had
when you were a kid
becomes a part of you when you grow up
permanently

homesick
for a home
you are not sure
exists.

there are some things in life so beautiful that you can do them over and over again without ever getting sick of it. like that cup of coffee you drink every morning without fail. or how fascinating it feels every time you see the sky turn pretty colors. or the conversations you have with the right people. the people you can talk to about anything at any time and you just never seem to run out of things to talk about.

but what kind of life is this, really
if I can't do the thing
I want the most.

I'm not sure if it's possible to be fully certain of something you have never done before. I mean – all you have is a vision, right? there is no way you can tell if this vision will come true or not. you can do all the reading, all the talking to people, all the internal debates you have with yourself, and maybe that makes it a little easier. but at the end of the day, you still gotta take that leap. and there is still a possibility that you might hurt yourself in the process. but there will always be that little resistance in you. that little voice in your head telling you that maybe you should reconsider it. but you have already reconsidered it plenty of times. you are trying to wait for that absolute certainty. but deep down, you know that it is not going to come. I think at the end of it all, it comes down to one question – *how much do you really want it?*

I think that makes all the difference.

there is still
so much
left in me
I can't wait to get out.

I want to be excited for what life has to offer. I think there is a lot out there. things we know. and more that we don't. I want to be able to be in a situation and feel completely satisfied by it. I know satisfaction is largely a mindset, but I want to be in a place so satisfactory that I won't even begin to wonder about it. I just think there is a lot in life and I wonder if I'll ever be able to cling onto enough to be truly happy about.

there is hope
in the things
that have not
happened yet.

3 things I've learned from solo traveling the first time:

1. no matter how much you prepare, there will always be this tiny reluctance to leave. but that tiny reluctance will disappear once you leave.

2. nothing will go completely to plan. nothing. the best plan is to react to whatever comes along.

3. every good thing is momentary. every bad thing is momentary. when the trip is over, everything else you did is just a memorable experience. you can't get attached to those moments. but you can always create more memories.

I think everyone should solo
travel at least once in their lives.

do it
with all your heart
or don't do it at all.

I've done some things in my life
the same ones people told me
were "too good to be true"
and funny enough,
I think the hardest part of it all
was convincing myself
that I deserved it
and went after the things I wanted
instead of the things I should
and somehow,
that was the biggest contributing factor.

— *self-belief*

you never know
how far you can go
until you decide
to give it a go.

how to change your life:

buy a one-way plane ticket

take a step out.

you don't have to do it all at once.

but take one little step. it makes all the difference.

you reach a point in life where you find yourself doing the same things and getting the same results.

same old thing over and over again. and over time, your life starts to come to a standstill.

this is where taking a step out makes all the difference.

it doesn't have to be big. it doesn't have to be significant. it just has to be different. and that tiny difference will be all you need to propel you forward.

the fear of change is not what usually stops you from growing. it is the desire to actually want to move forward. and making the effort to do it.

one little step. by one little step. that's all you need.

how much
do you actually
want it?

it makes all the difference.

you have come too far
to still be doubting
your own capabilities.

picture this. you're up early and it's quiet outside. the only sounds you hear are birds from far away, and the cold, crisp air blowing at you. you make a hot cup of coffee and you sit outside. it is too cold but you take your blanket out and you do it anyway. the view is beautiful and the world is calm. inside, you're at peace. there isn't anything else you want to do at the moment. there isn't anywhere else you need to be. you drink your coffee and you think about how just a year ago, where you are now seemed like a lifetime away. you are still not where you want to be, not yet. but you no longer feel hopeless and the void that was once inside your heart doesn't seem to be there anymore. you take another sip of coffee. it warms you up from the inside. the trust you have in the process seems to be stronger than ever.

no idea
where I want to be
but I will keep going.

drink more coffee
stay for sunsets
create more,
and fuck things up
a little more often.

who are you
when you are not addicted
by all the internet stimulation

who are you
when you stop doing things
for instant gratification

who are you
when you stop trying so hard
just to get validation

who are you
when no one
is watching you?

all it takes is one.

the answers

you need

are in you

pick a direction
and start moving,
the rest will come.

take your own advice.

we have become so good at comforting others.

that we often forget to comfort ourselves
when we need it the most.

the advice you need is already in you.

listen to yourself.

the answers you need
are really just the same ones,
over and over again.

— *consistency*

you don't know
what you want
but you know
what you don't want
and that is a damn good place
to start.

you gotta embrace your circumstances. you are where you are right now. there is nowhere else you could be in this moment. you can get lost in the idea of where you want to be in the future all you want, but it doesn't change the fact that you are here right now and nowhere else. accept what you can't control. embrace where you are. and keep working on what you know you gotta do to get yourself to where you want to be.

keep chasing after
what you have in mind
one day
it will all make sense.

the simplest
and hardest thing
you can do for yourself
is to do the things
exactly as you say you would.

you glow differently when you stop
giving a fuck about what others think.

someone asked me this question the other day:

do you ever feel like you're wasting time and not
actually living, almost like you're waiting to live?

this is a question I relate to a lot. growing up, I've
always felt this way. I've lived my entire life desperately
wishing I was somewhere else, doing something
else. waiting for my life to start happening.

as I got older, I realized that my life is already
happening. it's a mindset thing. waiting is a
choice – one that leads to nothing changing.

I couldn't wait anymore. I was desperate for things to
change and I wanted it to happen immediately. and
it's interesting. because the moment you start to "take
control" of the situation, things start to change.

change can happen very quickly. but not always
for the better. or at least not immediately.
but change is good. especially when you are
tired of your constant. any change is good.

embracing change creates opportunities. and
opportunities create hope. and hope will bring
you the momentum you need to keep going.

the truth is – you are often more "in
control" than you think you are.

make a decision
and the universe
will align
accordingly.

whatever you do,
never forget
your initial intention.

if you don't
pick yourself up,
who will?

you've done it once. you can do it again.

whatever you need to get through,
you already have it in you.

and you know that.

I know it feels hard sometimes.

you don't know if you want to keep trying.
because it feels like you keep ending back up in
the same place. so what's the point of trying?

but it won't always be like this.

I can't say better. because I really
don't know if there is better.

but I know different. I've seen plenty of
different. sometimes they are the same
thing. and occasionally, they are not.

it's the hope that keeps us going.

most people will not want
the same things you want
as badly as you
and that is
your superpower.

you take the chances
you think you deserve.

I can't control
what the universe
does to me
but I can control
how I react accordingly

sometimes the universe
throws shit at me
and I go through it
and become a better person

sometimes the universe
throws shit at me
and it hits me flat on my face
and I shrug it off
and walk away
because choosing
to be a bigger person
is easier than dealing with shit
you don't want to deal with

sometimes the universe
throws shit at me
and I simply dodge it.
because I'm not a fucking tree
and I am mobile

but regardless
the universe
does what the universe does
and I am merely
a particle in its entirety

stop telling yourself no.

when your heart says yes.

stop talking yourself out of things you want the most.

you deserve good things.

you deserve to have things you actually want.

let yourself move towards where you want to be.

one conversation can change your life.

we tell people
the things we want to hear
but never had the courage
to say it to ourselves
and call it advice.

there is so much
we try to say
in the things
we don't say.

a concept: just do whatever the fuck you want and feels right. even if it doesn't work out as well as it could if you plan it, you will end up being happier and that's better.

if it's meant to be,
it will come back.

you have to believe that things will get better. you have to believe that change is possible. you have to believe that you have the power you need in you, because you do. you have to believe that this path you're working towards will lead to somewhere, and even if you don't get to your end goal right away, you will still be so much further than where you were before.

you have to believe that things will work out, because they will, in due time. you have to believe in the process, because it is as much about commitment and effort as it is about being in the right direction. you have to believe in the possibility of good things happening to you, and accept the losses you have to take along the way. you have to believe that good will come out of it.

you have to believe in yourself. you have to believe that you will be able to figure it out, whatever difficulties you encounter. you have to believe in help. you have to believe in the people who try to help you, and trust that they have the best intentions in their hearts. you have to believe that sometimes people with the best intentions don't end up fitting with one another, and that it's okay if you outgrow them.

you have to just believe – you make a decision, and the universe will always align accordingly. you have to believe that life will always move forward as long as you continue to walk it. you have to believe in the destination and love the process, and believe that while you may not know where you will end up yet, it will be somewhere beautiful.

make your ideas come to life.

remember that one thing you thought you'd never be able to overcome but you did? yeah. you can do that again.

give yourself time.

whatever that means to you right now.

one day it will come
things will start to work out
and you won't see it coming
because you were too busy
working on yourself.

don't tell me what to do
I don't need your answers
they are not mine,
let me figure out
on my own.

whatever you need, you already have.

you don't need more to get started, you need to start.

the more you do, the luckier you will become.

everything you need to do the things you
want is already inside of you.

we all get older
and sometimes we forget
the things we said
we would do for ourselves
when we get older.

growth
is when you look back
at the things you wrote down
when you were younger
and realize
that you don't feel the same
anymore.

ron lim

maybe
who you are
is all you
will ever need
to become.

the end

hello :)

my name is ron. and if you are reading this, it means that I have successfully put together a whole book and figured out how to publish it. I know I will probably feel different about it by the time this book is in your hands, but as of right now in this moment as I'm writing this, the idea of me having a book that I can show to the world feels a little foreign. almost daunting, even.

fun fact – I never wanted to be nor cared about being a writer. but I did enjoy writing a lot. in the form of tweets in the early days of social media, and Instagram posts throughout recent years. I just never saw it as "writing". all I cared about was that putting all these writings out on the internet was fun, and it made me feel good. so I just kept on at it.

it's funny how life works out sometimes.

if you have read the entire book, I thank you for taking the time. this is the first time I tried writing a book, and doing so was a lot of fun.

I hope I can continue to write more of these.

– September, 2021

hello again :)

my name is still ron. and if you are reading this, it means that you have read the second edition of my book!

things are a little different now. I have a publisher and I no longer have to figure out how to do everything on my own. which I am very grateful for. I've sold a few thousand copies of my first edition book that I self-published in my first few months — which gave me the confidence to believe that maybe I can really become a writer after all.

my publishing team told me that I should write a different "author's note" for my second edition. but I thought I'd leave the first one in so you guys can see the process as it truly is.

one thing that has changed since I self-published my book is that I started introducing myself to new people I've met that I am a "writer". because I now have a book that people can buy and I no longer just post quotes on Instagram.

I know this is like the simplest thing, but I just never thought of myself as one. and it still feels weird for me to see myself that way, but I guess I technically am a writer now.

I like to talk about the process exactly as I do them. and rawness is not always the most aesthetic thing, but I think there is a special kind of connection you find within yourself when you keep it real. and also with others who do the same.

so this right here – is my process.

this is the second edition of my first book.

I am grateful for every person who bought my first edition –
which allowed this to happen.

I am grateful for every person who supported me on my jour-
ney – my non-stop traveling and my radical online content.

I am grateful for you who bought this book –
which allows my writing journey to continue.

this is only the beginning.

I have so many ideas and so much passion and I am con-
stantly looking for things I can channel my energy to. and I
will continue to talk about the process exactly as I do them.

thank you for being a part of my process.

– July, 2022

Instagram: @ronwritings
www.ronwritings.com

More from
Thought Catalog Books

How to Laugh in Ironic Amusement
During Your Existential Crisis
—*James McCrae*

The Mountain Is You
—*Brianna Wiest*

Somewhere In Between
—*Kelly Peacock*

Don't F*cking Panic
—*Kelsey Darragh*

THOUGHT
CATALOG
Books

THOUGHTCATALOG.COM